Pastry Chef

A Pastry Cookbook with Delicious Puff Pastry Recipes

By
BookSumo Press

Published by
http://www.booksumo.com

Table of Contents

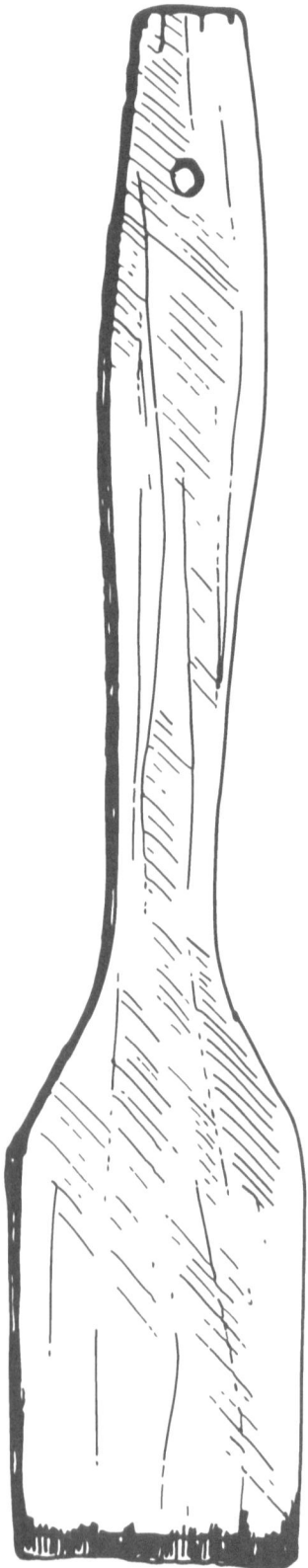

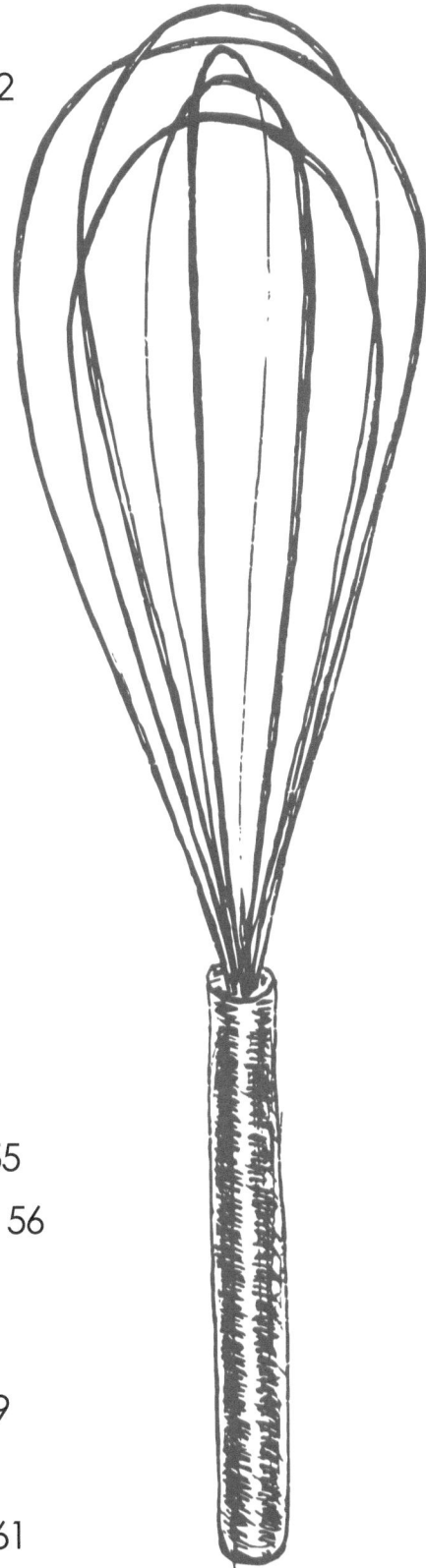

Creamy
Chicken Salad Cups

🥣 Prep Time: 20 mins
🕐 Total Time: 1 hr 30 mins

Servings per Recipe: 8
Calories	338 kcal
Fat	24.2 g
Carbohydrates	14.9 g
Protein	15.1 g
Cholesterol	154 mg
Sodium	414 mg

Ingredients

1 C. water
1/2 C. butter
1/8 tsp salt
1 C. all-purpose flour
4 eggs
1/4 C. red onion, chopped
1 stalk celery, chopped
1 tbsp raisins

2 tsp Dijon mustard
1/3 C. mayonnaise
1/4 C. plain yogurt
1/2 tsp salt
1/4 tsp dried dill weed
2 C. chopped cooked chicken breast

Directions

1. Before you do anything preheat the oven to 400 F. Spray a baking pan and place it aside.
2. Place a large saucepan over medium heat. Stir in it the Cook them until they start boiling. Add the flour and mix them well until your get a smooth ball of dough.
3. Turn off the heat and let it rest for 12 min. Add the eggs gradually after incorporating each one of them completely then stir them well until they become smooth.
4. Spoon the dough by heaping tbsp to make 8 mounds in total. Cook them in the oven for 34 min. Allow the puffs to lose heat completely.
5. Slice the tops of the puffs to make the caps leaving their inside empty and place them aside.
6. Get a large mixing bowl: Toss in it the onion, celery, raisins, mustard, mayonnaise, yogurt, 1/2 tsp salt, dill, and chopped chicken.
7. Spoon the mix into the inside of the puffs then cover them with their caps. Serve them right away.
8. Enjoy

CREAMY
Crab Exes

Prep Time: 20 mins
Total Time: 40 mins

Servings per Recipe: 18	
Calories	199 kcal
Fat	14.3 g
Carbohydrates	13.2g
Protein	4.9 g
Cholesterol	15 mg
Sodium	119 mg

Ingredients

2 tbsp olive oil
3 C. fresh chopped mushrooms
2 green onions, chopped
1 clove garlic, crushed
1/2 tsp ground cayenne pepper

4 oz cream cheese, softened
1 (6 oz) can crabmeat, drained and flaked
1 (17.5 oz) package frozen puff pastry sheets, thawed

Directions

1. Before you do anything preheat the oven to 400 F. Spray a baking pan and place it aside.
2. Place a saucepan over medium heat. Heat the oil in it. Add the mushrooms, green onions, garlic and cayenne pepper. Sauté them for 12 min.
3. Get a mixing bowl: Combine in it the veggies mix with cream cheese and crabmeat. Mix them well.
4. Flatten the pastry dough over a floured working surface in the shape of a 12x12 inches square. Slice into 4 inches squares.
5. Place 1 tbsp of the filling in the middle of each pastry squares. Pull the squares corners on top then pinch them in the middle. Transfer them to the baking pan.
6. Cook them in the oven for 22 min. Serve them warm.
7. Enjoy.

Italian Style
Tenderloin Packets

Prep Time: 20 mins
Total Time: 55 mins

Servings per Recipe: 4
Calories	1231 kcal
Fat	84.8 g
Carbohydrates	59.9g
Protein	45.6 g
Cholesterol	157 mg
Sodium	630 mg

Ingredients

4 (4 oz) beef tenderloin filets
2 tbsp olive oil
1 shallot, minced
1 tsp minced garlic, or to taste
1 C. broth
1 pinch garlic salt, or to taste
1 pinch Italian seasoning, or to taste

1 (8 oz) package cream cheese, softened
2 sheets frozen puff pastry, thawed
1 egg white (optional)
1/4 C. water (optional)

Directions

1. Before you do anything preheat the oven broiler. Place the oven rack 6 inches away from the heat. Transfer the beef tenderloin fillets to a roasting pan and broil the for 3 min on each side. Place them the fillets aside.
2. Before you do anything preheat the oven to 375 F.
3. Place a large pan over medium heat. Heat the oil in it. Add the garlic with shallot and cook them for 6 min.
4. Stir in the pinot noir and cook them for until they start boiling. Keep cooking it for 12 min while stirring from time to time. Add the garlic salt and Italian seasoning.
5. Lower the heat and fold in the cream cheese until the mix becomes smooth to make the sauce.
6. Roll a pastry sheet on a floured working surface. Slice it in half crosswise. Spread some of the cream cheese sauce on a pastry half then top it with a sirloin half.
7. Wrap the pastry sheet over the steak. Wet your hands and press the edges to seal them. Repeat the process with the remaining pastry half and the other pastry sheet.
8. Get a small mixing bowl: Mix in it the water with egg while. Spread it over the steak packets. Transfer them to greased baking sheets.
9. Cook them in the oven for 26 min. Serve your steak packets warm. Enjoy.

FAMOUS
White lasagna Bites

Prep Time: 20 mins
Total Time: 50 mins

Servings per Recipe: 12
Calories	406 kcal
Fat	24.6 g
Carbohydrates	30g
Protein	14 g
Cholesterol	38 mg
Sodium	695 mg

Ingredients

2 skinless, boneless chicken breast halves, cubed
3 tbsp chopped onion
3 cloves garlic, minced
3 C. fresh spinach
1 1/2 C. ricotta cheese
1/2 C. grated Parmesan cheese

6 tbsp butter, softened
3 (10 oz) cans refrigerated crescent roll dough

Directions

1. Before you do anything preheat the oven to 325 F.
2. Place a large pan over medium heat. Heat a splash of oil in it. Add the onion with garlic and chicken. Cook them for 6 min. Add the spinach and cook them for 12 min.
3. Get a mixing bowl: Place in it the spinach and chicken mix to lose heat for a while. Add the ricotta cheese, Parmesan cheese, and butter. Stir them well until they become creamy.
4. Lay the crescent rolls on a floured working surface. Wet your hands and bring each two crescent rolls together to make a rectangular. Pinch them to keep them sealed to make 12 in total.
5. Place 1 tbsp of the filling to the middle of each rectangular. Pull the pastry corners on top and seal them shaping them into balls.
6. Transfer them to a lined baking pan. Cook them in the oven for 13 min. Serve them warm.
7. Enjoy.

Hot
Coconut Chicken Squares

🥣 Prep Time: 30 mins
🕐 Total Time: 1 hr 5 mins

Servings per Recipe: 9

Calories	424 kcal
Fat	25.3 g
Carbohydrates	35.5g
Protein	14.2 g
Cholesterol	22 mg
Sodium	423 mg

Ingredients

1 tbsp vegetable oil
1/2 tsp ground coriander
1/2 tsp ground turmeric
1/2 tsp ground cumin
2 tsp curry powder
1/2 C. coconut milk, or more as needed
2 red onions, chopped
1 stalk lemon grass, thinly sliced

1 red chile pepper, roughly chopped
1 large russet potato, diced
3/4 lb skinless, boneless chicken breast, cut in bite-sized pieces
1 tsp salt
1 (17.25 oz) package frozen puff pastry, thawed

Directions

1. Place a large saucepan over medium heat. Heat the oil in it. Add the coriander, turmeric, cumin, and curry powder. Sauté them for 30 sec.
2. Stir in the coconut milk, onions, lemon grass, and red pepper. Cook them for 8 min. Add the potato and cook them for 14 min while adding more milk if needed.
3. Add the chicken with a pinch of salt and pepper. Cook them for 4 to 6 min. Place the filling aside to lose heat completely.
4. Before you do anything preheat the oven to 375 F. Cover two cookie sheets with some parchment papers.
5. Roll the pastry over a floured working surface. Slice each sheet into 9 squares. Divide the filling into the middle of each square.
6. Pull the pastry corners of each square on top and pinch them to seal them. Transfer them to the baking sheets. Cook them in the oven for 26 min. Serve them warm.
7. Enjoy.

PUFFY
Veggies Pouches

Prep Time: 5 mins
Total Time: 20 mins

Servings per Recipe: 12

Calories	215 kcal
Fat	11.6 g
Carbohydrates	19.8g
Protein	2.9 g
Cholesterol	16 mg
Sodium	66 mg

Ingredients

1 sheet frozen puff pastry
2 tbsp olive oil
1/2 tsp fresh shallots, minced
1 C. frozen corn
1 C. fresh mushrooms, chopped
1/4 C. broth
1/2 tsp white pepper
1/2 tsp dried thyme
3 C. fresh spinach
1 egg, beaten
Sauce:

1 tbsp olive oil
1/2 tsp fresh shallots, minced
1/4 C. celery, chopped
1 C. broth
3 tbsp brown sugar
1 bay leaf
2 tsp cold water
2 tsp cornstarch

Directions

1. Before you do anything preheat the oven to 375 F. Cover two cookie sheets with some parchment papers.
2. Roll the pastry on a floured working surface in the shape of 12 inches rectangular. Slice it into 12 squares.
3. Place a skillet over medium heat. Heat the oil in it. Add the shallots, corn, and mushrooms. Cook them for 2 min. Stir in the broth, seasonings, and spinach. Cook them for 1 min.
4. Turn off the heat and place the filling aside to lose heat slightly. Spoon 1 tbsp of the mix into each square. Coat the sides of the squares with the beaten egg.
5. Pull the corners of the squares in the middle on top then twist while pulling on top slightly. Transfer them to the lined cookie sheets.
6. Coat the veggies pouches with the rest of the beaten egg. Cook them in the oven for 19 min.
7. To make the sauce:
8. Place a skillet over medium heat. Heat the oil in it. Add the celery with shallot. Cook them

for 1 min. Stir in the broth, brown sugar, and bay leaf over high heat. Lower the heat to medium.

9. Get a small mixing bowl: Mix in it the cornstarch with water. Stir it into the pan and cook them for 6 min. Serve your sauce with your veggies pouches.

10. Enjoy.

PUFFY
Morel Lamb

Prep Time: 30 mins
Total Time: 1 hr

Servings per Recipe: 4

Calories	946 kcal
Fat	63.9 g
Carbohydrates	47.9 g
Protein	42.1 g
Cholesterol	212 mg
Sodium	2314 mg

Ingredients

1 tbsp olive oil
1 small shallot, minced
1/2 C. fresh morel mushrooms, sliced
1/2 C. fresh oyster mushrooms, stemmed and sliced
2 tbsp apple cider vinegar
1 tsp ground cumin
1 tsp paprika
1 tsp dried oregano
2 tsp brown sugar
1 tsp garlic powder

1 tsp dried parsley flakes
2 tsp ground black pepper
2 tsp kosher salt
1 rack of lamb, trimmed and frenched
1 sheet frozen puff pastry, thawed
2 egg yolk, beaten
3/4 C. demi-glace
2 tbsp butter
2 tbsp chopped fresh parsley

Directions

1. Place a large pan over medium heat. Heat the oil in it. Add the minced shallot, morel and oyster mushrooms. Sauté them over medium high heat for 4 min.
2. Stir in the apple cider. Place the mix aside to lose heat.
3. Get a small mixing bowl: Mix in it the cumin, paprika, oregano, brown sugar, garlic powder, parsley flakes, pepper, and salt. Massage the mix into the lamb rack.
4. Before you do anything preheat the oven to 350 F. Cover a baking sheet with a piece of foil and grease it.
5. Roll out the pastry over the baking sheet. Spread the mushroom mix on one side of it.
6. Place the rack of lamb on the top of it. Make a slice 2 inches away after the edges of the pastry.
7. Make a slit in the pastry between each lamb rack bone then pull the pastry strip over it to cover it and pull the second edges to seal it with the strips using some water stick them.
8. Coat the wrapped lamb with the beaten egg yolk and place it in the fridge for 12 min.

9. Transfer the wrapped rack of lamb over the baking sheet and cook it in the oven for 16 min. Allow it to rest for 6 min.

10. Pour the demi glace in a small saucepan and cook it until it starts simmering. Add the butter and mix them until it melts. Serve it with the lamb rack after slicing it.

11. Enjoy.

HABANERO
Cheese Wheels

Prep Time: 20 mins
Total Time: 34 mins

Servings per Recipe: 6
Calories	233 kcal
Fat	16 g
Carbohydrates	18.7g
Protein	3.4 g
Cholesterol	34 mg
Sodium	143 mg

Ingredients

1 egg yolk
2 tsp Dijon mustard
1 tsp water
1 sheet frozen pre-rolled puff pastry sheet

1 clove garlic, pressed
1/3 C. CRACKER BARREL Shredded Habanero Heat Cheese, divided

Directions

1. Before you do anything preheat the oven to 400 F. Cover a baking sheet with a piece of foil and grease it.
2. Get a mixing bowl: Combine in it the egg yolk, mustard and water. Mix them well. Add the garlic.
3. Flatten the pastry over a floured working surface in the shape of a 14x10-inch rectangle. Slice in half lengthwise. Spread on them some of egg yolk mix.
4. Spread 3 tbsp of cheese on a half of a pastry sheet. Top it with the second half then brushed side with egg facing down.
5. Roll the rectangular tightly and slice it into 2 circles. Lay them on the baking sheet and press them gently to flatten them. Top them with the rest of the cheese.
6. Cook them in the oven for 13 min. Serve them warm.
7. Enjoy.

Sweet
Cinnamon Wheels

🍲 Prep Time: 20 mins
🕐 Total Time: 1 hr

Servings per Recipe: 24
Calories	79 kcal
Fat	4.3 g
Carbohydrates	9.5g
Protein	0.7 g
Cholesterol	1 mg
Sodium	< 28 mg

Ingredients

1/4 C. white sugar
1 sheet frozen puff pastry, thawed
1 tbsp butter, melted
1/3 C. white sugar
3/4 tsp ground cinnamon

1/8 tsp ground cardamom
water

Directions

1. Before you do anything preheat the oven to 375 F.
2. Spread 1/4 C. of sugar on a working surface. Roll on it the pastry in the shape of a 15x10-inch rectangular. Spread on it some butter.
3. Get a small mixing bowl: Combine in it the 1/3 C. sugar, cinnamon, and cardamom. Spread the mix all over the rolled our pastry.
4. Dust your hands with flour and roll 1 long edge of the pastry tightly until your reach the center. Repeat the process with the other side of the pastry until it reaches the other folded half.
5. Brush between them with some butter and press them tightly. Cut the log into 1/4 inches slices and place them on a lined up baking sheet.
6. Cook them in the oven for 14 min. Allow them to cool down completely then serve them.
7. Enjoy.

VANILLA
Pie Shell

Prep Time: 40 mins
Total Time: 3 hrs

Servings per Recipe: 8
Calories   249 kcal
Fat   16.2 g
Carbohydrates   22.7g
Protein   3.4 g
Cholesterol   64 mg
Sodium   84 mg

Ingredients

1 1/2 C. all-purpose flour
3 tbsp white sugar
1/4 tsp salt
2/3 C. unsalted butter, cubed

1 egg, beaten
1/2 tsp vanilla extract

Directions

1. Get a mixing bowl: Mix in it the flour, sugar, and salt. Add the butter and mix them with your hands until the mix becomes coarse.
2. Pour the mix on a working surface and shape into a mount making a well in the middle of it. Place in it the egg with vanilla.
3. Whisk the egg gently with a fork while drawing the flour mix into the inside until you mix all the flour. Use a pastry blender to mix them again well.
4. Shape the mix back into a mound. Get 2 to 3 tbsp of the mix on a side of working surface and sweep it with your hand. Repeat the process with the rest of the flour mix.
5. Mix the dough again and repeat the process of sweeping small portions of it twice.
6. Dust your hands with flour and knead the dough 6 times with your hand until it becomes smooth. Flatten it into a 5 inches circle.
7. Dust the dough circle with some flour and place it a piece of plastic wrap over it to cover it. Chill it in the fridge for 22 min. Place it aside to rest for 10 in the kitchen.
8. Flatten the dough until it becomes 1/8 inches thick. Place the rolling pin inches away from the edges of dough and pull it on top of it.
9. Keep rolling the rolling pine with the dough towards you.
10. Transfer the dough to a greased baking pie pan and un-roll it gently while pressing it to the bottom of the pan and lifting the dough from the edges to prevent it from being torn.
11. Use a scissors to remove the excess of the pastry from the sides and place the pie shell in the freezer for 32 min.

12. Before you do anything preheat the oven to 425 F.

13. Draw gently a circle that is bigger than the pie pan with 2 inches in the middle of a 12 inches piece of foil. Grease it with butter.

14. Place the butter side facing the bottom of the crust and hanging from the sides. Cover the bottom of the pie shell with dry beans enough to make a thin layer.

15. Cook it in the oven for 19 min. Allow the pie shell to rest for 30 sec. Discard the beans and foil piece.

16. Lower the oven to 375 F. Cook the pie shell in the oven for 4 min. Remove the pie gently from the pan and place it aside to cool down.

17. Fill the crust with your favorite filling then serve it.

18. Enjoy.

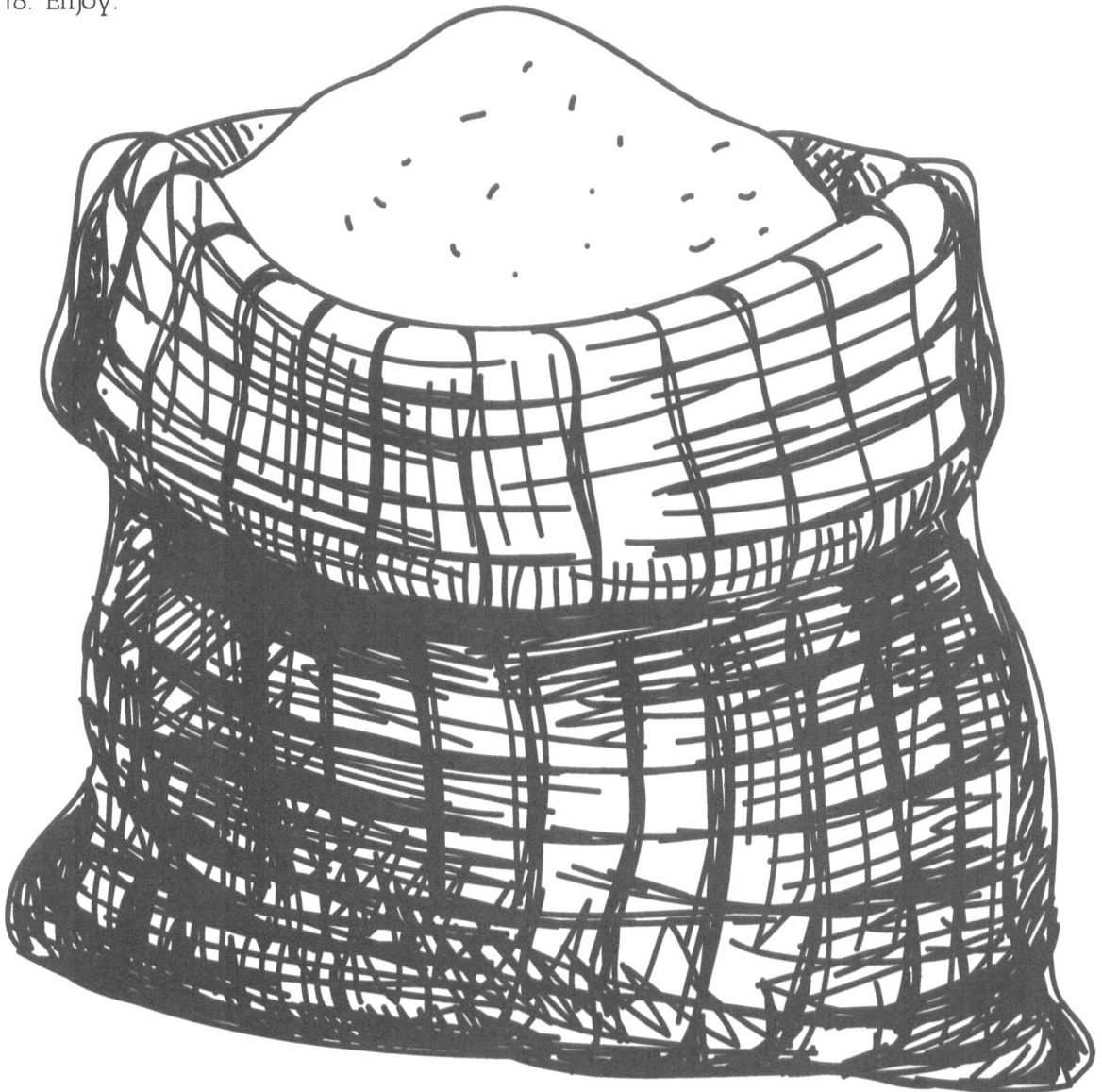

CHEESE
Worms

Prep Time: 20 mins
Total Time: 1 hr

Servings per Recipe: 24
Calories	121 kcal
Fat	8.3 g
Carbohydrates	9.4g
Protein	2.3 g
Cholesterol	1 mg
Sodium	79 mg

Ingredients

1/2 C. Parmesan cheese
3/4 tsp ground black pepper
1/2 tsp garlic powder
1 (17.5 oz) package frozen puff pastry, thawed

1 egg white

Directions

1. Before you do anything preheat the oven to 350 F.
2. Get a small mixing bowl: Stir in it the parmesan cheese, pepper and garlic powder.
3. Roll out the pastry sheets on a floured working surface. Spread on them some egg white. Spread on them the parmesan cheese mix equally and press it gently with your hands.
4. Slice the pastry sheets into 12 strips each and twist them gently. Place them on a lined up baking sheet and cook them in the oven for 16 min. Serve them warm.
5. Enjoy.

Blue Pears
Puffs

Prep Time: 35 mins
Total Time: 2 hrs

Servings per Recipe: 36

Calories	109 kcal
Fat	7.4 g
Carbohydrates	9.2g
Protein	1.8 g
Cholesterol	5 mg
Sodium	91 mg

Ingredients

3 tbsp butter
1 tbsp olive oil
4 sweet onions, thinly sliced
1 (17.5 oz) package frozen puff pastry, thawed

salt and pepper to taste
2 firm pears, peeled, quartered, and sliced
3/4 C. crumbled blue cheese

Directions

1. Before you do anything preheat the oven to 375 F. Cover 2 cookie sheets with some parchment paper.
2. Place a large pan over medium heat. Heat in it the olive oil with butter. Add the onion and sauté it for 35 min until it caramelizes over low heat while stirring it often.
3. Season the caramelized onion with some salt and pepper.
4. Roll out the pastry on a floured working surface. Slice each pastry sheet into 9 squares and each square into 2 triangles.
5. Place the triangles on the lined up baking sheet. Top them with some of the caramelized onion, pear slices and 1 tsp of blue cheese of each triangle.
6. Cook them in the oven for 28 min. Allow them to lose heat completely then serve them.
7. Enjoy.

PUFFY
Bell Crawfish Tails Pie

Prep Time: 20 mins
Total Time: 2 hrs 20 mins

Servings per Recipe: 12

Calories	411 kcal
Fat	29.3 g
Carbohydrates	23.2g
Protein	15.7 g
Cholesterol	122 mg
Sodium	460 mg

Ingredients

1 C. butter
1/2 C. flour
1 sweet onion , chopped
1 green bell pepper, chopped
celery, chopped
4 green onions, chopped
1/2 C. vegetable broth
2 lb cooked and peeled whole crawfish tails

3 tbsp tomato paste
3 cloves garlic, chopped
1/4 C. fresh parsley, chopped
salt and ground black pepper to taste
cayenne pepper to taste
hot sauce to taste
12 puff pastry shells

Directions

1. Place a large pan over medium heat. Heat the butter in it. Add the flour and mix them. Cook them until the flour mix becomes golden brown.
2. Stir in the sweet onion, green pepper, celery, and green onions. Put on the lid and cook them for 1 h over low heat while stirring often.
3. Add the broth with tomato paste. Stir them well. Stir in the crawfish tails, garlic, and parsley. Cook them for 16 min. Stir in the salt, black pepper, cayenne pepper, and hot sauce.
4. Before you do anything preheat the oven to 400 F. Cover 2 cookie sheets with some parchment paper.
5. Place the pastry shells on a lined up baking sheet. Cook them in the oven for 6 min. Place them aside to lose heat for a while.
6. Remove the caps of the shells and place them aside. Lower the oven heat to 350 F.
7. Divide the filling over the pastry shells. Place them on the baking sheet. Pour the rest of the filling in a small greased baking pan. Place the shells caps over it to cover it.
8. Cook them in the oven for 16 min. Serve them warm. Enjoy

Almond
Cream Stuffed Ring

Prep Time: 1 hr 50 mins
Total Time: 1 hr 50 mins

Servings per Recipe: 12
Calories	321 kcal
Fat	25.3 g
Carbohydrates	19.7g
Protein	4.5 g
Cholesterol	137 mg
Sodium	142 mg

Ingredients

1/2 C. butter
1/4 tsp salt
1 C. water
1/4 C. blanched slivered almonds
1 C. all-purpose flour
4 eggs
2 C. heavy cream
1 C. confectioners' sugar

2 tsp vanilla extract
1/4 tsp almond extract

Directions

1. Before you do anything preheat the oven to 400 F.
2. Place a heavy saucepan over medium high heat. Stir in it the butter, salt, water and almonds. Cook them until they start boiling. Add the flour and stir them well until you get a dough ball.
3. Turn off the heat and add one egg at a time while stirring them well. Pour the dough piping bag and pipe in the shape of 8 inches circle.
4. Cook the pastry circle in the oven for 52 min. Place it aside to lose heat completely.
5. Get a mixing bowl: Beat in it the cream, sugar, vanilla and almond extracts until they become smooth. Place the mix in the fridge for 1 h 10 min.
6. Beat the cream mix with an electric mixer until it soft peaks.
7. Slice the pastry ring in half to make two circles. Place the bottom circle on a serving plate and spread the cream mix over it. Top it with the upper ring half.
8. Dust your stuffed pastry ring with confectioners' sugar then serve it.
9. Enjoy.

SMOKED
Cod Packet

Prep Time: 30 mins
Total Time: 55 mins

Servings per Recipe: 4
Calories   602 kcal
Fat   40.6 g
Carbohydrates   30.3g
Protein   29.6 g
Cholesterol   138 mg
Sodium   382 mg

Ingredients

1 (1 lb) fillet cod
1/4 C. butter
2 tbsp chopped onion
2 3/4 C. fresh mushrooms, chopped
salt and black pepper to taste

4 1/2 oz smoked salmon pate
2 tbsp heavy cream
1 sheet frozen puff pastry, thawed
1 egg, beaten

Directions

1. Before you do anything preheat the oven to 425 F.
2. Use a sharp knife to cut the cod fillet in half and make 2 thin fillets of it.
3. Place a pan over medium heat. Heat the butter in it. Add the mushroom with onion and sauté them for 6 min. Stir in a pinch of salt and pepper. Place the mix aside to lose heat.
4. Get a mixing bowl: Combine in it the cream with salmon pate. Beat them until they become smooth. Fold in the mushroom and onion mix.
5. Flatten the pastry over a floured surface in the shape of a 12x14 inch rectangle. Put a cod fillet in the middle of it.
6. Spread on top of it half of the mushroom mix followed by a cod fillet and the rest of the mushroom mix. Fold the dough edges on top and pinch them to seal them.
7. Transfer the fish packet to a lined up baking sheet with the sealed side facing down. Spread the beaten egg on top of it. Cook in it in the oven for 28 min. Serve it warm.
8. Enjoy.

Butterscotch
Flat Apple Pie

Prep Time: 20 mins
Total Time: 50 mins

Servings per Recipe: 8
Calories	474 kcal
Fat	28.4 g
Carbohydrates	50g
Protein	5.8 g
Cholesterol	4 mg
Sodium	169 mg

Ingredients

flour for dusting
1 (17.5 oz) package frozen puff pastry
sheets (2 sheets), thawed
water, as needed
6 small tart apples - peeled, cored, and
sliced thinly
1 1/2 tsp ground cinnamon
1 tbsp brown sugar

1/4 C. toasted slivered almonds
1/4 C. butterscotch chips
1 tbsp butter, melted
1/2 tsp white sugar

Directions

1. Before you do anything preheat the oven to 375 F. Cover a baking sheet with a piece of parchment paper.
2. Roll two pastry sheets on a floured working surface next to each other. Wet your fingers and seal their short edges together to make a rectangular.
3. Get a mixing bowl: Toss in it the apple slices, cinnamon, brown sugar, almonds, and butterscotch chips.
4. Pour the mix in one half of the pastry rectangular. Fold the other half over it and seal its edges using some water.
5. Use a sharp knife and make several slits in the flat pie. Spread its top with the melted butter.
6. Place the flat pie gently in the baking sheet. Cook it in the oven for 16 min. Dust it with some sugar and cook it for 18 min in the oven. Serve it after it cools down slightly.
7. Enjoy.

FRUITY
Purple Chicken Pie

Prep Time: 25 mins
Total Time: 1 hr 15 mins

Servings per Recipe: 6

Calories	461 kcal
Fat	28.9 g
Carbohydrates	28.1g
Protein	22.1 g
Cholesterol	69 mg
Sodium	244 mg

Ingredients

1 sheet frozen puff pastry, thawed
1 lb cooked chicken meat, shredded
4 purple plums - pitted, peeled and chopped
3 tbsp chicken broth
1/2 tsp ground allspice
1/4 tsp ground cinnamon
salt and freshly ground black pepper to taste

1 pinch ground cloves
2 purple plums, pitted and sliced
2 tbsp melted butter
1 tbsp light brown sugar

Directions

1. Before you do anything preheat the oven to 375 F. Cover a baking pie pan with a piece of parchment paper.
2. Roll the pastry sheet on a floured surface. Transfer to the pastry sheet and press it gently. Trim the excess dough.
3. Get a large mixing bowl: Toss in it the chicken, 4 chopped plums, chicken broth, allspice, cinnamon, and cloves, salt and pepper.
4. Pour the mix in the pie pan and lay on it the plum slices. Pour the melted butter on top followed by the brown sugar. Cook the pie in the oven for 42 min. Serve it warm.
5. Enjoy.

Flat Smoked
Paprika and Salmon Packet

Prep Time: 20 mins
Total Time: 1 hr 18 mins

Servings per Recipe: 4
Calories	1206 kcal
Fat	85.7 g
Carbohydrates	60.8g
Protein	47.8 g
Cholesterol	132 mg
Sodium	653 mg

Ingredients

2 tbsp olive oil, divided
1/2 onion, chopped
1 C. chopped fresh mushrooms
2 tsp minced garlic, divided
salt and ground black pepper to taste
1 C. baby spinach
1 tbsp all-purpose flour, or as needed
2 sheets frozen puff pastry (such as Pepperidge Farm(R)), thawed
1 (1 1/2-lb) boned, skinned salmon fillet

1/2 tsp smoked paprika, or more to taste
1 egg, beaten
Sauce:
1/2 C. mayonnaise
2 tbsp fresh lemon juice
2 tsp Dijon mustard
1/2 tsp dried dill

Directions

1. Before you do anything preheat the oven to 350 F. Cover a baking pan with a piece of parchment paper.
2. Place a large pan over medium heat. Heat 1 tbsp of olive oil in it. Add the onion and cook it for 6 min. Stir in the mushrooms and 1 tsp garlic. Cook them for 6 min.
3. Place the mix in a mixing bowl and place it aside. Heat 1 tbsp of oil in the same pan. Cook in it 1 tsp of garlic for 40 sec. Add the spinach and cook them for 4 min.
4. Season them with some salt and pepper. Place it aside to lose heat.
5. Roll the pastry sheet on a floured working surface. Spoon the mushroom mix into it and spread it evenly leaving 1/2 inch of the edges empty.
6. Place the salmon in the center and top it with the spinach. Wrap the pastry on top and pinch the edges to seal them. Transfer the salmon packet to the baking sheet.
7. Spread the beaten egg on it. Cook it in the oven for 44 min. Allow it to rest for 6 min.
8. Get a small mixing bowl: Mix in it the mayonnaise, lemon juice, Dijon mustard, and dill to make the sauce. Serve it with the salmon packet. Enjoy.

BLUE SAUSAGES
and Grapes Braid

🍳 Prep Time: 30 mins
🕐 Total Time: 1 hr 15 mins

Servings per Recipe: 12

Calories	364 kcal
Fat	24.6 g
Carbohydrates	27g
Protein	9.5 g
Cholesterol	47 mg
Sodium	341 mg

Ingredients

olive oil
4 links apple-chicken sausage, diced
2 C. diced sweet potatoes
2 stalks celery, diced
1/2 C. diced red onion
1/2 C. diced red bell pepper
2 cloves garlic, chopped
salt and ground black pepper to taste
1 C. seedless green grapes, halved

1 (3 oz) package cream cheese, softened
1/2 C. crumbled blue cheese, or more to taste
1 tsp dried rosemary, crushed
2 sheets frozen puff pastry, thawed
1 tbsp sliced almonds, or as needed (optional)

Directions

1. Before you do anything preheat the oven to 350 F. Cover a baking pan with a piece of parchment paper.
2. Place a large pan over medium heat. Heat the oil in it. Add the apple-chicken sausage, sweet potatoes, celery, red onion, red bell pepper, and garlic. Cook them for 17 min.
3. Get a mixing bowl: Place in it the sausage and veggies mix with a pinch of salt and pepper. Fold in the grapes.
4. Add the cream cheese, blue cheese, and rosemary. Stir them well.
5. Roll the pastry sheets on the baking sheet and flatten them. Pinch their edges to make them into 1 long rectangular.
6. 3 inches away from the both the long edges of the pastry, make 1 1/2 inch strips leaving the middle of the both short sides intact.
7. Spoon the chicken mix into the center of the pastry and spread it. Use the strips on the sides to create a braid over the filling to cover it. Sprinkle the almonds on top.
8. Cook the stuffed braid in the oven for 32 min. Serve it warm.
9. Enjoy.

Summer
Cheese Squares

Prep Time: 20 mins
Total Time: 50 mins

Servings per Recipe: 8
Calories	468 kcal
Fat	33.8 g
Carbohydrates	31.1g
Protein	11 g
Cholesterol	18 mg
Sodium	324 mg

Ingredients

2 tbsp olive oil
1 C. chopped green onions
2 cloves garlic, minced
1 (5 oz) creamy goat cheese log
1/2 C. grated Parmesan cheese
1 pinch cayenne pepper, or more to taste
2 sheets frozen puff pastry, thawed
1/2 lb zucchini, thinly sliced
1/2 lb roma tomatoes, thinly sliced

salt and ground black pepper to taste
1 tsp olive oil, or as needed
2 tbsp thinly sliced basil leaves

Directions

1. Place a large pan over medium heat. Heat 2 tbsp of olive oil in it. Add the green onion and cook it for 4 min. Stir in the garlic and cook them for 2 min. Turn off the heat.
2. Get a small mixing bowl: Mix in it the goat cheese, Parmesan cheese, and cayenne pepper.
3. Roll the pastry sheet on a floured working surface. Slice each sheet into 4 squares and make slit 1/4 inch away from its edges.
4. Before you do anything preheat the oven to 350 F.
5. Cover a two baking sheets with a piece of parchment paper. Place the dough squares on them. Top them with the cheese mix followed by the onion mix.
6. Place the squares in the fridge for 8 min. Top it with the zucchini and tomato slices while overlapping them. Sprinkle some salt and pepper on top then pour 1 tsp of olive oil on each one.
7. Cook them in the oven for 22 min. Serve them warm with some basil strips for garnish.
8. Enjoy.

NUTTY
Puff Sticks

Prep Time: 15 mins
Total Time: 30 mins

Servings per Recipe: 36
Calories	82 kcal
Fat	5.7 g
Carbohydrates	6.5g
Protein	1.3 g
Cholesterol	0 mg
Sodium	52 mg

Ingredients

1/2 C. Parmesan cheese
1 (17.5 oz) package frozen puff pastry, thawed
1 egg white, beaten

1/3 C. finely chopped shelled pistachios
kosher salt to taste

Directions

1. Before you do anything preheat the oven to 350 F.
2. Roll out the pastry sheets on a floured surface. Spread the egg white over them. Top them with some the pistachios and some kosher salt.
3. Flip the pastry sheet and repeat the process on the other side. Slice them into 3 inches long and 3/4 inches wide strips. Twist them gently and place them on lined baking sheet.
4. Cook them in the oven for 16 min. Allow them to cool down completely. Serve them with your favorite dip or dessert.
5. Enjoy.

Cheesy
Mushroom Puffs

Prep Time: 20 mins
Total Time: 35 mins

Servings per Recipe: 2
Calories	630 kcal
Fat	50.9 g
Carbohydrates	31.1g
Protein	14.2 g
Cholesterol	73 mg
Sodium	458 mg

Ingredients

1/2 sheet puff pastry
3 tbsp butter
1/4 lb mushrooms, sliced
2 cloves garlic, crushed
1/2 C. crumbled goat cheese

4 tsp finely chopped fresh parsley

Directions

1. Before you do anything preheat the oven to 400 F. Coat a baking sheet with a cooking spray and place it aside.
2. Roll the pastry over a floured surface and slice it into 8 squares. Pierce the squares several times with a fork. Transfer them to the baking tray.
3. Cook them in the oven for 8 min. Press the squares with the back of a metal spatula. Cook them for 7 min in the oven again.
4. Place a pan over medium heat. Heat the butter in it. Add the garlic with mushroom, a pinch of salt and pepper. Cook them for 6 min.
5. Spoon the mix over the puff squares and top them with the goat cheese and parsley. Serve them.
6. Enjoy.

FANCY
Flat Beef Pies

Prep Time: 35 mins
Total Time: 1 hr 55 mins

Servings per Recipe: 2

Calories	3274 kcal
Fat	215.3 g
Carbohydrates	232.4g
Protein	68.7 g
Cholesterol	196 mg
Sodium	1359 mg

Ingredients

1 tsp olive oil
2 (6 oz) beef tenderloin filets
1 tbsp butter
8 oz fresh white mushrooms, minced
1/3 C. minced shallot
2 cloves garlic, minced
2 tbsp apple cider

4 6-inch squares of frozen puff pastry, thawed but still cold
1 1/2 C. broth
salt and pepper to taste
1 egg (optional)
2 tbsp milk (optional)

Directions

1. Place a heavy pan over medium heat. Heat the oil in it. Add the beef fillets and cook them for 3 min on each side. Place them in the oven for 1 h.
2. Heat the butter in the same pan. Cook in it the mushrooms, shallot, and garlic for 7 min. Add 2 tbsp of apple cider and stir them to scrap the brown bites.
3. Pour the mix in a bowl and place it in the fridge for 48 min.
4. Roll two pastry sheets on a floured working surface. Place a beef fillet over each one and top them with the cooked mushroom mix.
5. Cover them with a second sheet of pastry. Wet your fingers and seal the edges of the pastry. Use a sharp knife to make 2 slits on each beef packet.
6. Place a heavy saucepan over medium heat. Pour in it 1 1/2 C. of broth. Cook it for 16 min until it reduces by half. Stir in the some salt and pepper to make the sauce.
7. Before you do anything preheat the oven to 450 F. Coat a baking sheet with a cooking spray and place it aside.
8. Get a mixing bowl: Mix in the milk with egg. Use a brush to spread the mix over the beef packets. Transfer them to the baking sheet.
9. Cook them in the oven for 16 min. Sere them warm with the broth sauce.
10. Enjoy.

Curried
Veggie Pot Pie

🥣 Prep Time: 20 mins

🕐 Total Time: 1 hr

Servings per Recipe: 8

Calories	518 kcal
Fat	31.6 g
Carbohydrates	52.5g
Protein	7.4 g
Cholesterol	13 mg
Sodium	356 mg

Ingredients

1 3/4 C. sweet potato, peeled and cut into 2-inch chunks
1 3/4 C. red potatoes, peeled and cut into 2-inch chunks
1 3/4 C. parsnips, peeled and cut into 2-inch chunks
1 3/4 C. carrots, peeled and cut into 2-inch chunks
2 tbsp olive oil
sea salt and ground black pepper to taste

1 tbsp butter
1 C. chopped onion
2 tbsp butter
1 1/2 C. vegetable broth
1/2 C. whole milk
3 tbsp all-purpose flour
1 1/2 tsp curry powder
1 (17.25 oz.) package frozen puff pastry, thawed and cut into four 5-inch squares

Directions

1. Set your oven to 400 degrees F before doing anything else.
2. In a roasting pan, add the sweet potato, red potatoes, parsnips, carrots, olive oil, sea salt and black pepper and toss to coat well.
3. Cook in the oven for about 20-30 minutes.
4. In a pan, melt 1 tbsp of the butter on medium heat and cook the onion for about 3-5 minutes.
5. Add the sweet potato mixture, 2 tbsp of the butter, salt and black pepper and cook for about 2-3 minutes.
6. In another pan, heat the vegetable broth and milk on medium heat,
7. Stir in the flour and curry powder till well combined.
8. Slowly, add the broth mixture and cook for about 3 minutes, stirring continuously.
9. Divide mixture into 4 pot pie dishes and top each with a puff pastry square.
10. Cook in the oven for about 17-20 minutes.

OLD-FASHIONED
Turkey Pot Pie

Prep Time: 45 mins
Total Time: 1 hr 25 mins

Servings per Recipe: 8

Calories	502 kcal
Fat	31.6 g
Carbohydrates	39.6 g
Protein	16 g
Cholesterol	69 mg
Sodium	868 mg

Ingredients

2 C. all-purpose flour
1 tsp salt
7 tbsp cold vegetable shortening
6 tbsp cold butter
6 tbsp cold water
3 tbsp butter
2 carrots, diced
1 onion, diced
2 stalks celery, diced
1/8 tsp ground black pepper
2 tbsp all-purpose flour

2 C. cubed cooked turkey
2 tbsp butter
2 C. chicken broth
1 (15 oz.) can cut green beans, drained
1 (10.75 oz.) can condensed cream of mushroom soup
1/2 (15 oz.) can cream-style corn
1 tbsp chopped fresh flat-leaf parsley
1 tbsp chopped fresh thyme

Directions

1. In a bowl, mix together 2 C. of the flour and salt.
2. With a pastry cutter, cut in the vegetable shortening and 6 tbsp of the cold butter till the butter and shortening are the size of small peas.
3. Sprinkle with the cold water, 1 tbsp at a time and with a fork gently, mix till a non-sticky dough is formed.
4. Divide the dough into 2 equal-sized pieces and shape each into a round.
5. Refrigerate till using.
6. Set your oven to 425 degrees F.
7. In a large skillet, melt 3 tbsp of the butter on medium heat and cook the carrots, onion, celery and black pepper for about 8 minutes.
8. Transfer the mixture into a bowl and keep aside.
9. In a resealable plastic zipper bag, place 2 tbsp of flour and cooked turkey meat.
10. Seal the bag and shake the to coat.

11. In the same skillet, melt 2 tbsp of the butter on medium heat and cook the turkey meat for about 10 minutes.
12. Add the chicken broth, 1/2 C. at a time and bring to a simmer, stirring occasionally.
13. Cook for about 5 minutes, stirring occasionally.
14. Remove from the heat and stir in the cooked vegetables, green beans, cream of mushroom soup, cream-style corn, parsley and thyme till well combined.
15. Place each dough piece onto a floured surface and roll into a 11-inch circle.
16. Place the crust into a 10-inch pie dish and press to fit.
17. Place the filling into the bottom of crust and cover with the second crust.
18. Pinch the edges to seal the filling.
19. Cut 5 slits into the top crust.
20. Cook in the oven for about 15 minutes.
21. Now, set your oven to 350 degrees F and cook for about 25 minutes more

SEAFOOD
Sampler Pot Pie

Prep Time: 15 mins
Total Time: 1 hr 25 mins

Servings per Recipe: 6
Calories	587 kcal
Fat	33.1 g
Carbohydrates	46.7g
Protein	25.8 g
Cholesterol	119 mg
Sodium	1058 mg

Ingredients

1 (3 oz.) package dry crab boil
5 small lobster tails
1 (15 oz.) package double crust ready-to-use pie crust
5 tbsp butter
1/2 C. diced onion
1/2 C. diced celery
1/3 C. all-purpose flour
1 1/2 C. chicken broth
3/4 C. milk
1 tsp seafood seasoning

1/2 tsp garlic powder
1/4 tsp freshly ground black pepper
1 1/2 C. frozen mixed vegetables, thawed
1/2 C. diced potato

Directions

1. Set your oven to 425 degrees F before doing anything else.
2. In a large pan, add the water and crab boil and bring to a boil.
3. Stir in the lobster tails and boil for about 5-8 minutes.
4. Drain and cool the lobster tails.
5. Remove shells and chop the lobster meat.
6. Transfer the lobster meat into a bowl.
7. Place a pie crust in the bottom of a 9-inch pie pan and press to fit.
8. In a skillet, melt the butter on medium heat and cook the onion and celery for about 5-8 minutes.
9. Add the flour and stir to combine well.
10. In a bowl, mix together the chicken broth and milk.
11. Slowly, add the broth mixture into the onion mixture, stirring continuously till thickened.
12. Add the seafood seasoning, garlic powder and ground black pepper and stir to combine

well.

13. Stir in the thawed vegetables, diced potato and cooked lobster meat and simmer for about 8 minutes.

14. Place the lobster mixture into the prepared pie crust and cover with the remaining pie crust.

15. Crimping the edges to seal the filling.

16. With a sharp knife, cut an 'X' into top of pie crust.

17. Cook in the oven for about 40 - 45 minutes.

18. Remove from the oven and keep aside to cool for about 10 - 15 minutes before serving.

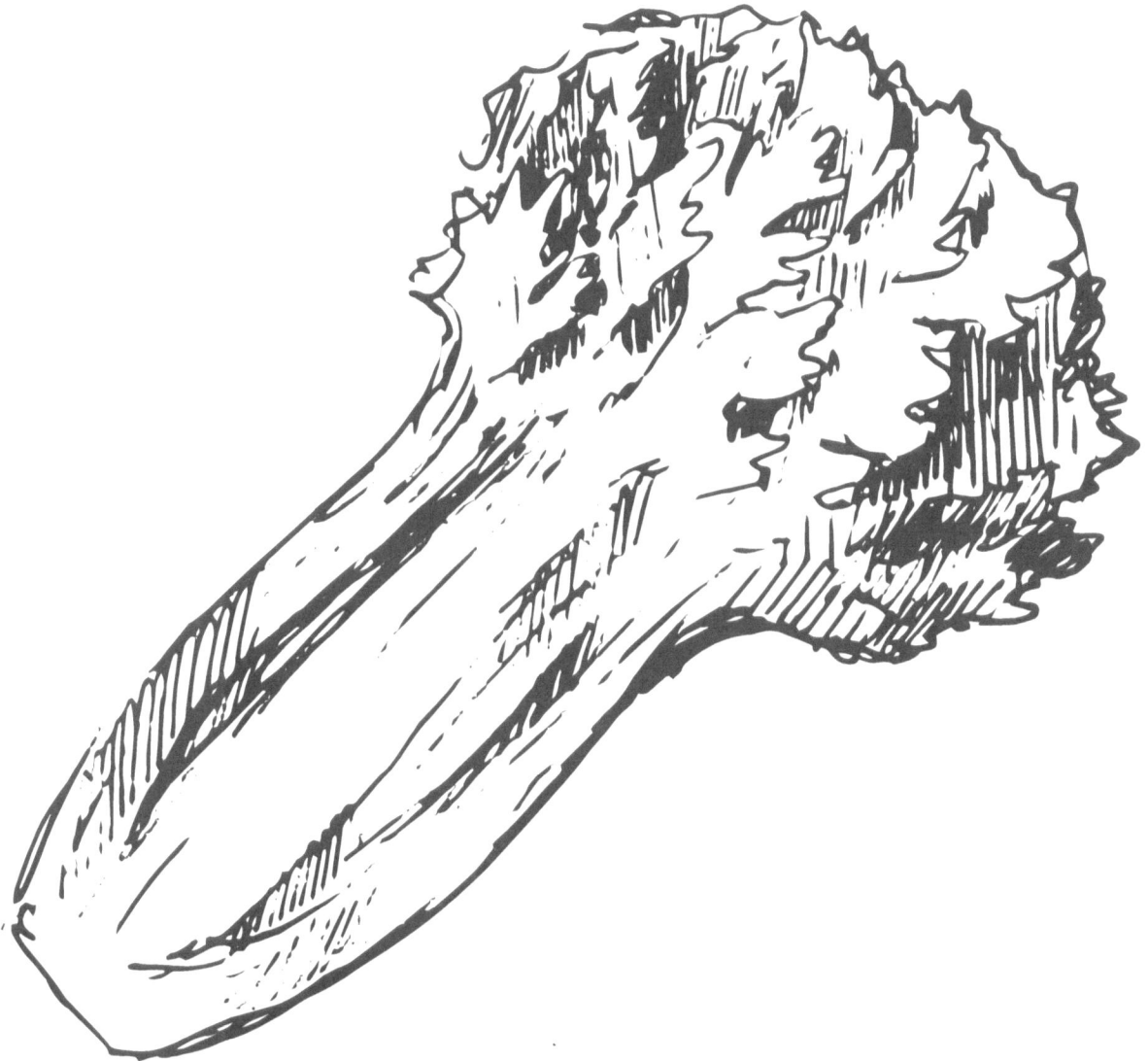

NOVEMBER'S
Pot Pie

Prep Time: 20 mins
Total Time: 1 hr 40 mins

Servings per Recipe: 6

Calories	563 kcal
Fat	32.4 g
Carbohydrates	45.9 g
Protein	21.7 g
Cholesterol	52 mg
Sodium	513 mg

Ingredients

1 (15 oz.) package pastry for a 10-inch double crust pie
2 tsp canola oil
1 small onion, minced
2 carrots, diced
1 stalk celery, finely chopped
2 tbsp dried parsley
1 tsp dried oregano
salt and ground black pepper to taste
1 tbsp butter
2 C. low-sodium chicken broth

1 C. peeled and cubed sweet potato
1 C. frozen green peas
1 tbsp butter
2 C. cubed cooked turkey
3 tbsp all-purpose flour
2/3 C. milk
1 stalk celery, finely chopped

Directions

1. Set your oven to 425 degrees F before doing anything else.
2. Place the pie crust pastry into the bottom of a 10-inch pie dish and press to fit.
3. In a large skillet, heat the oil on medium heat and cook the onion, carrots, celery, parsley, oregano, salt and black pepper for about 5 minutes.
4. Stir in 1 tbsp of the butter till melted.
5. Add the chicken broth and bring to a boil.
6. Stir in the sweet potato and simmer for about 15 minutes.
7. Stir in the peas and reduce the heat to low.
8. In a pan, melt the remaining 1 tbsp of the butter on medium-low heat and cook the turkey and flour for about 5 minutes.
9. Add the milk and bring to a gentle boil.
10. Transfer the turkey mixture into the vegetable mixture and cook for about 10 minutes.
11. Remove from the heat and keep aside to cool.

12. Cook the bottom crust in the oven for about 8 minutes.

13. Remove from the oven and keep aside to cool for about 5 minutes.

14. Place the turkey mixture into crust and cover with the remaining crust.

15. Pinch the edges to seal the filling.

16. Cut four slits in the top crust.

17. Cook in the oven for about 15 minutes.

18. Now, set your oven to 350 degrees F and cook for about 10 minutes more.

TURKEY
& Potato Pot Pie

Prep Time: 20 mins
Total Time: 1 hr 10 mins

Servings per Recipe: 12

CCalories	490 kcal
Fat	27 g
Carbohydrates	40.1g
Protein	20.3 g
Cholesterol	40 mg
Sodium	782 mg

Ingredients

1 tbsp olive oil
1 3/4 C. diced onions
1 tsp minced garlic
1 (26 oz.) can cream of chicken soup
1/4 C. broth
2 tsp ground black pepper
1 tsp herbes de Provence
1 tsp poultry seasoning
1/2 tsp dried oregano

1/4 tsp dried basil
salt to taste
4 C. cubed cooked turkey
1 1/4 C. diced potatoes
1 C. frozen peas
1 C. diced carrots

Directions

1. Set your oven to 425 degrees F before doing anything else.
2. In a deep skillet, heat the oil on medium heat and cook the onions and garlic for about 5 minutes.
3. Add the cream of chicken soup, broth, black pepper, herbes de Provence, poultry seasoning, oregano, basil and salt and bring to a simmer.
4. Remove from the heat and gently, stir in the turkey, potatoes, peas and carrots.
5. Place 2 pie crusts into two 9-inch pie dishes and press to fit.
6. Place the filling into the pie crusts evenly and top each with a second pie crust.
7. Pinch the edges to seal the filling.
8. Cut several slits in the top crust of each pie.
9. Cook in the oven for about 30-35 minutes.
10. Remove from the oven and keep aside to cool for about 10 minutes before serving.

Zesty
Italian Pot Pie

🥣 Prep Time: 20 mins

🕐 Total Time: 50 mins

Servings per Recipe: 6

Calories	283 kcal
Fat	12.5 g
Carbohydrates	24.8g
Protein	18.1 g
Cholesterol	39 mg
Sodium	449 mg

Ingredients

1 lb. boneless skinless chicken breasts, cut into bite-size pieces
1/4 C. KRAFT Lite Zesty Italian Dressing
4 oz. PHILADELPHIA Neufchatel cheese, cubed
2 tbsp flour
1/2 C. fat-free reduced-sodium chicken broth

3 C. frozen mixed vegetables (peas, carrots, corn, green beans), thawed, drained
1/2 (15 oz.) package ready-to-use refrigerated pie crust

Directions

1. Set your oven to 375 degrees F before doing anything else.
2. Heat a large skillet on medium heat and cook the chicken in dressing for about 2 minutes.
3. Add the Neufchatel and cook for about 3-5 minutes.
4. Stir in the flour till well combined.
5. Stir in the broth and vegetables and simmer for about 5 minutes.
6. Place the mixture into a 10-inch deep-dish pie plate and cover with a pie crust.
7. Crimp and flute the edge.
8. Cut slits in top crust.
9. Cook in the oven for about 30 minute

AMERICAN
Chicken Pot Pie

Prep Time: 5 mins
Total Time: 35 mins

Servings per Recipe: 6
Calories	209 kcal
Fat	8 g
Carbohydrates	22g
Protein	12.4 g
Cholesterol	57 mg
Sodium	622 mg

Ingredients

1 2/3 C. frozen mixed vegetables
1 C. cut-up cooked chicken
1 (10.75 oz.) can condensed cream of
chicken soup

1 C. Bisquick mix
1/2 C. milk
1 egg

Directions

1. Set your oven to 400 degrees F before doing anything else.
2. In an 9x1-1/4-inch ungreased glass pie plate, mix together the vegetables, chicken and soup.
3. In a bowl, add the remaining ingredients and with a fork, mix till well combined.
4. Place the mixture into pie plate and cook in the oven for about 30 minutes.

Chicken
& Corn Pot Pie

Prep Time: 10 mins
Total Time: 55 mins

Servings per Recipe: 6

Calories	469 kcal
Fat	24.5 g
Carbohydrates	48g
Protein	13.9 g
Cholesterol	40 mg
Sodium	458 mg

Ingredients

1 (15 oz.) box refrigerated pie crusts, softened as directed on box
1 (9 oz.) pouch creamy roasted garlic with chicken stock cooking sauce
1/4 C. all-purpose flour
1/2 tsp poultry seasoning
1 (12 oz.) bag frozen mixed vegetables, thawed and drained
1 1/2 C. chopped deli rotisserie chicken

Directions

1. Set your oven to 425 degrees F before doing anything else.
2. Prepare the pie crusts according to box's directions for Two-Crust Pie.
3. Place a crust into 9-inch glass pie plate and press to fit.
4. In a bowl, add the cooking sauce, poultry seasoning, 1/2 tsp of the salt and 1/4 tsp of the pepper and mix till smooth.
5. Add the chicken and vegetables and stir to combine.
6. Place the filling mixture into the bottom crust and cover with the second crust.
7. Crimp the edges and flute.
8. Cut several slits in the top crust.
9. Cook in the oven for about 20 minutes.
10. Now, cover the edge of crust with strips of foil and cook in the oven for about 10 minutes.
11. Remove from the oven and keep aside to cool for about 10 minutes before serving

LOUISIANAN
Pot Pie

Prep Time: 45 mins
Total Time: 2 hrs 5 mins

Servings per Recipe: 8
Calories	840 kcal
Fat	48.1 g
Carbohydrates	60.5g
Protein	38.2 g
Cholesterol	194 mg
Sodium	1572 mg

Ingredients

1/4 C. canola oil
1 (16 oz.) package turkey kielbasa sausage, cut into 1 inch pieces
1 lb. cooked chicken meat, shredded
2 tbsp Cajun seasoning, divided
2 tbsp Cajun blackened seasoning, divided
1 onion, chopped
3 stalks celery, chopped
1 large green bell pepper, chopped
1/4 C. all-purpose flour

2 quarts chicken broth
1 1/2 C. uncooked white rice
1 lb. uncooked medium shrimp, peeled and deveined
1 tbsp ground black pepper
1 tbsp cayenne pepper
2 (9 inch) prepared pie crusts
1 beaten egg

Directions

1. Set your oven to 375 degrees F before doing anything else.
2. In a large pan, heat the canola oil on medium heat and cook the kielbasa sausage and chicken meat for about 10 minutes.
3. Stir in 1 tbsp of the Cajun seasoning and 1 tbsp of blackened seasoning and transfer the sausage mixture into a bowl.
4. In the same pan, add the onion, celery, bell pepper and 1 tbsp of the Cajun seasoning and 1 tbsp of blackened seasoning and cook for about 5 minutes.
5. With a slotted spoon, transfer the vegetables into a bowl and keep aside.
6. For the roux: in the same pan, add the flour on low heat and beat till well combined with the oil.
7. Cook for about 15 minutes, stirring occasionally.
8. Slowly, add the chicken broth, 1/2 C. at a time, stirring continuously and bring to a gentle boil.

9. Stir in the cooked sausage, chicken and vegetables and cook for about 20 minutes, stirring occasionally.
10. Stir in the rice and simmer for about 15 minutes; mix in the shrimp and cook until they are opaque and pink, 5 to 10 minutes.
11. Stir in the black pepper and cayenne pepper and remove from the heat.
12. Place a pie crust into a 9-inch pie dish and press to fit.
13. Coat the crust with the beaten egg and with a fork, poke the holes into all over the crust.
14. Cook in the oven for about 3 minutes.
15. Place the filling mixture over the baked crust and cover with the second crust.
16. Pinch and crimp the edges and coat the crust with the beaten egg.
17. Cut several slits into the top of the crust.
18. Cook in the oven for about 10-15 minutes.
19. Cover the edges of the crust with a piece of the foil and cook in the oven for about 5 minute

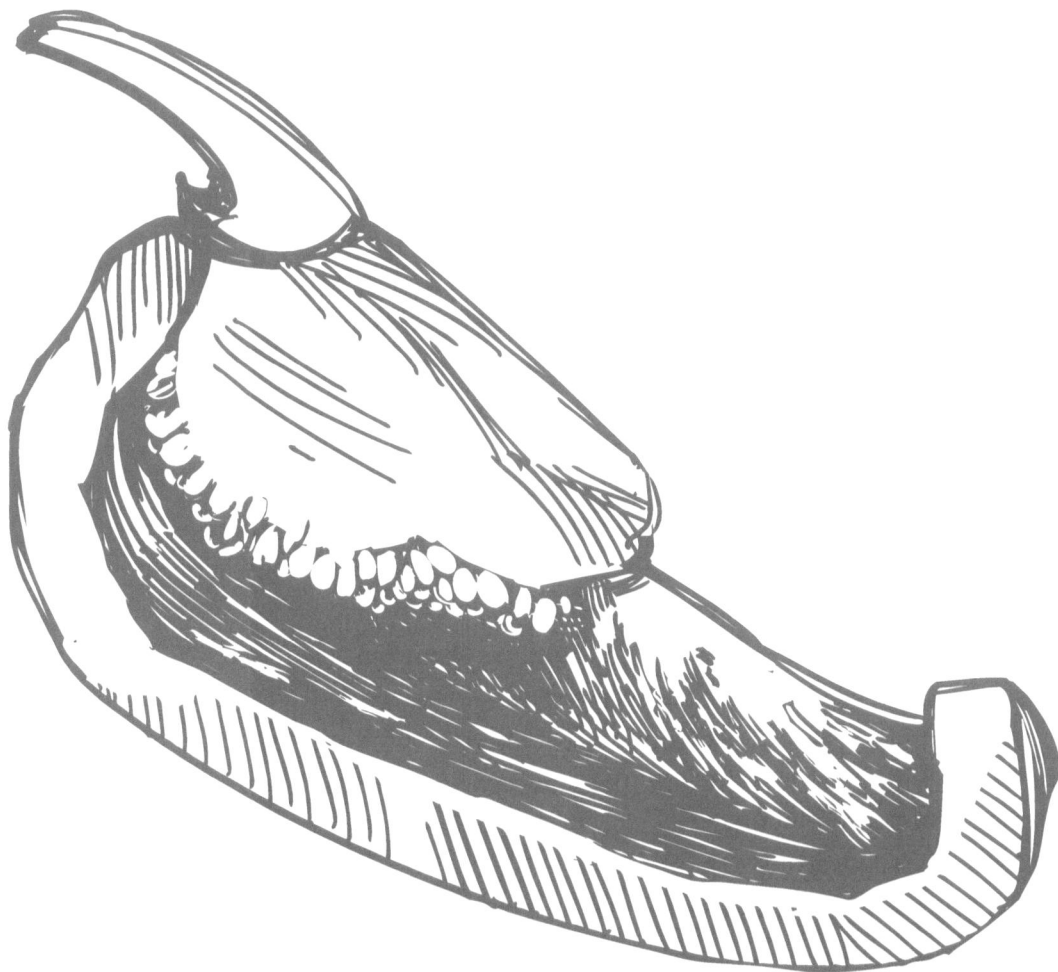

TURKEY
Sage Pot Pie

Prep Time: 30 mins
Total Time: 1 hr 20 mins

Servings per Recipe: 8

Calories	463 kcal
Fat	25 g
Carbohydrates	31.7g
Protein	27.1 g
Cholesterol	78 mg
Sodium	795 mg

Ingredients

1/4 C. canola oil
1 1/2 C. all-purpose flour
1/2 tsp salt
1/2 C. vegetable shortening
1/4 C. water
1/4 C. butter
1/4 C. all-purpose flour
1 tsp salt
1/2 tsp ground black pepper
1 tsp rubbed sage
1 C. chicken broth

1 C. evaporated milk
4 C. cooked turkey, cut into bite-size pieces
2 (15 oz.) cans mixed vegetables, drained

Directions

1. Set your oven to 425 degrees F.
2. In a bowl, mix together 1 1/2 C. of the flour and 1/2 tsp of the salt.
3. With a pastry cutter, cut the shortening into the flour mixture till crumbly.
4. Slowly, add the water, 1 tbsp at a time and mix till just dough holds together.
5. Divide the dough in 2 equal sized portions.
6. Place each portion onto a floured surface and with a rolling pin, roll into an 11-inch circle.
7. Place 1 crust into a 10-inch pie dish and press to fit.
8. In a bowl, mix together 1/4 C. of the flour, sage, 1 tsp of the salt and black pepper.
9. In a large pan, melt the butter on medium heat and cook the flour mixture till a smooth paste is formed, stirring continuously.
10. Cook for about 1 minute, stirring continuously.
11. Stir in the chicken broth and evaporated milk and bring to a boil, stirring continuously.
12. Cook for about 2 minutes.

13. Remove the sauce from the heat and stir in the cooked turkey meat and mixed vegetables.

14. Place the filling mixture into the prepared pie dish and cover with the remaining crust.

15. Pinch and fold together the edges of the crusts to seal the filling.

16. With a sharp knife, cut an X into the center of the top crust.

17. Cook in the oven for about 35-40 minutes.

18. Remove from the oven and keep aside to cool for 10 minutes before serving.

OMEGA-3
Pot Pie

Prep Time: 20 mins
Total Time: 1 hr 5 mins

Servings per Recipe: 5
Calories	565 kcal
Fat	45.5 g
Carbohydrates	25.1g
Protein	15.2 g
Cholesterol	153 mg
Sodium	784 mg

Ingredients

3 C. clam juice
1 (3 oz.) salmon fillet, skin removed
1 tbsp olive oil
2 tbsp butter
1 carrot, peeled and diced
1 stalk celery, diced
1 small leek, diced
1 shallot, minced
3 tbsp all-purpose flour
1 C. heavy whipping cream
3 tbsp chopped fresh dill

1/2 lemon, juiced
salt and ground black pepper to taste
10 medium shrimp, peeled and deveined
1 1/2 oz. smoked salmon, chopped
1/2 sheet frozen puff pastry, thawed

Directions

1. Set your oven to 425 degrees F and grease 2 (2-C.) baking dishes.
2. In a small pan, add the clam juice and bring to a gentle boil.
3. Add the salmon fillet and poach for about 10 minutes.
4. Transfer the salmon onto a plate, reserving the poaching liquid.
5. In a skillet, heat the olive oil and butter on medium heat and cook the carrot, celery, shallots and leek for about 5 minutes.
6. Stir in the flour and cook for about 5 minutes.
7. Stir in the reserved poaching liquid and cream and simmer for about 3 minutes, stirring occasionally.
8. Stir in the dill, lemon juice, salt and pepper and remove from the heat.
9. with a spoon, break the salmon fillet into bite-sized pieces.
10. Divide the salmon pieces into the prepared baking dishes evenly and top with 1/3 the sauce.

11. Place 5 shrimp into each dish and top with 1/3 of the the sauce.

12. Now, place smoked salmon into each dish evenly and top with remaining 1/3 of the sauce.

13. Place the puff pastry sheet on a lightly floured surface and roll into 1/8-inch thickness.

14. Cut 2 pastry circles large enough to cover the baking dishes.

15. Place 1 circle over each filling in baking dishes.

16. Arrange the dishes onto a baking sheet and cook in the oven for about 15 minutes.

17. Remove from the oven and keep aside to cool for about 5 minutes before serving.

CREAMY FISH
Pot Pie

Prep Time: 10 mins
Total Time: 1 hr 20 mins

Servings per Recipe: 6
Calories   183 kcal
Fat   4.6 g
Carbohydrates   10.7g
Protein   23.4 g
Cholesterol   87 mg
Sodium   735 mg

Ingredients

1 tbsp vegetable oil
1 1/2 lb. mahi mahi fillets
1 tsp dried thyme
salt and ground black pepper to taste
1 (10.75 oz.) can condensed cream of
potato soup

1/2 C. milk
1 (15 oz.) can mixed vegetables (with
potatoes), drained
2 (9 inch) deep dish pie crusts

Directions

1. Set your oven to 375 degrees F before doing anything else.
2. Season the mahi mahi fillets with the thyme, salt and black pepper.
3. In a large skillet, heat the vegetable oil on medium heat.
4. Place the seasoned fillets and cook, covered for about 7 minutes per side.
5. Transfer the mahi mahi onto a cutting board and cut into bite-size pieces, removing bones.
6. In a pan, add the cream of potato soup, milk, mixed vegetables, salt and pepper on medium heat and simmer for about 5 minutes, stirring occasionally.
7. Gently, fold in the the mahi mahi pieces.
8. Place 1 prepared pie crust into a 9-inch deep-dish pie plate and press to fit.
9. Place the soup mixture into the pie crust and cover with the top crust.
10. Crimp the edges to seal the filling.
11. Cook in the oven for about 40-45 minutes.
12. Remove from the oven and keep aside to cool out for about 10-15 minutes before serving.

New York
Deli Pot Pie

Prep Time: 10 mins
Total Time: 55 mins

Servings per Recipe: 6
Calories	469 kcal
Fat	24.5 g
Carbohydrates	48g
Protein	13.9 g
Cholesterol	40 mg
Sodium	458 mg

Ingredients

1 (15 oz.) box refrigerated pie crusts, softened as directed on box
1 (9 oz.) pouch creamy roasted garlic with chicken stock cooking sauce
1/4 C. all-purpose flour
1/2 tsp poultry seasoning

1 (12 oz.) bag frozen mixed vegetables, thawed and drained
1 1/2 C. chopped deli honey turkey

Directions

1. Set your oven to 425 degrees F before doing anything else.
2. Prepare the pie crusts according to box's directions for Two-Crust Pie.
3. Place a crust into 9-inch glass pie plate and press to fit.
4. In a bowl, add the cooking sauce, poultry seasoning, 1/2 tsp of the salt and 1/4 tsp of the pepper and mix till smooth.
5. Add the honey turkey and vegetables and stir to combine.
6. Place the filling mixture into the bottom crust and cover with the second crust.
7. Crimp the edges and flute.
8. Cut several slits in the top crust.
9. Cook in the oven for about 20 minutes.
10. Now, cover the edge of crust with strips of foil and cook in the oven for about 10 minutes.
11. Remove from the oven and keep aside to cool for about 10 minutes before serving.

CANADIAN
Cream Pot Pie

Prep Time: 5 mins
Total Time: 45 mins

Servings per Recipe: 6	
Calories	380 kcal
Fat	21.1 g
Carbohydrates	40.8g
Protein	6.1 g
Cholesterol	35 mg
Sodium	873 mg

Ingredients

1 (15 oz.) can mixed vegetables, drained
1/2 C. milk
1/2 tsp dried thyme
1/2 tsp ground black pepper

2 (9 inch) frozen prepared pie crusts, thawed
1 egg, lightly beaten

Directions

1. Set your oven to 375 degrees F before doing anything else.
2. In a bowl, add the mushroom soup, milk, mixed vegetables, thyme and black pepper and mix well.
3. Place the filling in the bottom pie crust and cover with the top crust.
4. Crimp the edges to seal and cut several slits into the top crust.
5. Coat the top crust with the beaten egg.
6. Cook in the oven for about 40 minutes.
7. Remove from the oven and keep aside to cool for about 10 minutes before serving

Turkey
& Muenster Pot Pie

🥣 Prep Time: 25 mins
🕐 Total Time: 1 hr 30 mins

Servings per Recipe: 8

Calories	370 kcal
Fat	22.9 g
Carbohydrates	25.8g
Protein	14.7 g
Cholesterol	39 mg
Sodium	579 mg

Ingredients

1 1/2 C. chicken stock
1 C. cooked, shredded turkey
3/4 C. green peas
1/3 C. diced celery
1/3 C. diced carrots
1 1/2 C. shredded Muenster cheese

2 tbsp cornstarch
1/4 C. milk
1 recipe pastry for a 9 inch double crust pie

Directions

1. In a bowl, dissolve the cornstarch into milk.
2. In a medium pan, add the stock, turkey, carrots, peas and celery and bring to a boil.
3. Stir in the cornstarch and milk and cook for about 5 minutes, stirring continuously.
4. Remove from the heat and keep aside to cool for about 1 hour.
5. Set your oven to 325 degrees F.
6. Add the cheese into filling mixture and stir to combine.
7. Place the filling mixture into a 9-inch pie crust and cover with the second crust.
8. Crimp the edges and cut slits in top crust.
9. Arrange onto a baking sheet and cook in the oven for about 35-40 minutes

PORTUGUESE
Pasta Pot Pie

Prep Time: 10 mins
Total Time: 40 mins

Servings per Recipe: 4

Calories	703 kcal
Fat	37.7 g
Carbohydrates	51.3g
Protein	30.9 g
Cholesterol	60 mg
Sodium	2055 mg

Ingredients

3/4 lb. beef sausage, broken into small pieces
1 (15 oz.) jar spaghetti sauce with mushrooms
1 (15 oz.) can cannellini beans, drained and rinsed

1/2 tsp dried thyme
1 1/2 C. shredded mozzarella cheese
1 (8 oz.) package crescent roll dough, unrolled and divided into triangles

Directions

1. Set your oven to 425 degrees F before doing anything else.
2. Heat an oven proof skillet on medium heat and cook the sausage for about 12-15 minutes, until fully done.
3. Drain excess grease from the skillet.
4. Stir in the spaghetti sauce, beans and thyme and bring to a gentle boil.
5. Simmer for about 5 minutes.
6. Remove from the heat and stir in the cheese till melted completely.
7. Arrange crescent roll dough triangles on top of the beef sausage mixture in a spiral pattern with points of dough toward the center, covering the chorizo mixture completely.
8. Cook in the oven for about 12 minutes

52   Portuguese Pasta Pot Pie

Hudson River
Pot Pie

🥣 Prep Time: 10 mins
🕐 Total Time: 1 hr 20 mins

Servings per Recipe: 6
Calories	183 kcal
Fat	4.6 g
Carbohydrates	10.7g
Protein	23.4 g
Cholesterol	87 mg
Sodium	735 mg

Ingredients

1 tbsp vegetable oil
1 1/2 lb. tilapia fillets
1 tsp dried tarragon
salt and ground black pepper to taste
1 (10.75 oz.) can condensed cream of mushroom soup

1/2 C. milk
1 (15 oz.) can mixed vegetables (with potatoes), drained
2 (9 inch) deep dish pie crusts

Directions

1. Set your oven to 375 degrees F before doing anything else.
2. Season the tilapia fillets with the tarragon, salt and black pepper.
3. In a large skillet, heat the vegetable oil on medium heat.
4. Place the seasoned fillets and cook, covered for about 7 minutes per side.
5. Transfer the tilapia onto a cutting board and cut into bite-size pieces, removing bones.
6. In a pan, add the cream of mushroom soup, milk, mixed vegetables, salt and pepper on medium heat and simmer for about 5 minutes, stirring occasionally.
7. Gently, fold in the tilapia pieces.
8. Place 1 prepared pie crust into a 9-inch deep-dish pie plate and press to fit.
9. Place the soup mixture into the pie crust and cover with the top crust.
10. Crimp the edges to seal the filling.
11. Cook in the oven for about 40-45 minutes.
12. Remove from the oven and keep aside to cool out for about 10-15 minutes before serving.

BROOKLYN
Pastrami Pot Pie

Prep Time: 10 mins
Total Time: 55 mins

Servings per Recipe: 6
Calories	469 kcal
Fat	24.5 g
Carbohydrates	48g
Protein	13.9 g
Cholesterol	40 mg
Sodium	458 mg

Ingredients

1 (15 oz.) box refrigerated pie crusts, softened as directed on box
1 (9 oz.) pouch creamy roasted garlic with chicken stock cooking sauce
1/4 C. all-purpose flour
1/2 tsp poultry seasoning

1 (12 oz.) bag frozen mixed vegetables, thawed and drained
1 1/2 C. chopped deli pastrami

Directions

1. Set your oven to 425 degrees F before doing anything else.
2. Prepare the pie crusts according to box's directions for Two-Crust Pie.
3. Place a crust into 9-inch glass pie plate and press to fit.
4. In a bowl, add the cooking sauce, poultry seasoning, 1/2 tsp of the salt and 1/4 tsp of the pepper and mix till smooth.
5. Add the pastrami and vegetables and stir to combine.
6. Place the filling mixture into the bottom crust and cover with the second crust.
7. Crimp the edges and flute.
8. Cut several slits in the top crust.
9. Cook in the oven for about 20 minutes.
10. Now, cover the edge of crust with strips of foil and cook in the oven for about 10 minutes.
11. Remove from the oven and keep aside to cool for about 10 minutes before serving.

Spinach
and Pesto Open Pie

Prep Time: 15 mins
Total Time: 35 mins

Servings per Recipe: 2
Calories	685 kcal
Carbohydrates	38.9 g
Cholesterol	55 mg
Fat	43.7 g
Protein	33.5 g
Sodium	529 mg

Ingredients

2 (12 oz) skinless, boneless salmon fillets
seasoned salt to taste
1/2 tsp garlic powder
1 tsp onion powder
1 (17.25 oz) package frozen puff pastry, thawed

1/3 C. pesto
1 (6 oz) package spinach leaves

Directions

1. Set your oven at 375 degrees F before doing anything else.
2. Coat salmon with a mixture of salt, onion powder and garlic powder before setting it aside.
3. Now place ½ of your spinach between two separate puff pastry sheets, while putting more in the center and place salmon fillet over each one in the center before placing pesto and remaining spinach.
4. Moisten up the edges with water and fold it.
5. Bake this in the preheated oven for about 25 minutes.
6. Cool it down.
7. Serve.

ALMOND
nd Cheese Puff Pastry

wok Prep Time: 5 mins
clock Total Time: 25 mins

Servings per Recipe: 8
Calories   281 kcal
Carbohydrates   14.5 g
Cholesterol   28 mg
Fat   21 g
Protein   8.7 g
Sodium   255 mg

Ingredients

1/2 (17.5 oz) package frozen puff
pastry, thawed
1 (8 oz) wheel Brie cheese
1/4 C. sliced almonds

Directions

1. Set your oven at 350 degrees F before doing anything else.
2. Put puff pastry on the baking dish and place one half of horizontally sliced brie over it before spreading almonds and placing other half of brie on top.
3. Cover it up with pastry dough.
4. Bake this in the preheated oven for about 20 minutes.
5. Cool it down.
6. Serve.

Vineyard
Puff Pastry

Prep Time: 15 mins
Total Time: 1 hr 5 mins

Servings per Recipe: 16

Calories	68 kcal
Carbohydrates	5.1 g
Cholesterol	31 mg
Fat	3.2 g
Protein	3.3 g
Sodium	111 mg

Ingredients

2 eggs
2/3 C. all-purpose flour
1/2 C. broth
2/3 C. milk
1/2 tsp salt
1 green onion, chopped

3/4 C. shredded Swiss cheese
1 tbsp butter, melted
2 tbsps grated Parmesan cheese

Directions

1. Set your oven at 425 degrees F before doing anything else.
2. Pour a mixture of flour, broth, milk, salt, green onion, Swiss cheese, beaten eggs and butter in the baking dish before sprinkling some parmesan cheese.
3. Bake this in the preheated oven for about 35 minutes or until golden brown.
4. Cool it down.
5. Serve.

LEBANESE STYLE
Pot Pie

Prep Time: 4 hrs 15 mins
Total Time: 4 hrs 50 mins

Servings per Recipe: 4

Calories	515 kcal
Carbohydrates	33.6 g
Cholesterol	101 mg
Fat	32.6 g
Protein	22.4 g
Sodium	524 mg

Ingredients

3 tbsps mashed garlic
1 egg yolk
2 C. chopped fresh spinach
2 boneless skinless chicken breast halves
2 tbsps basil pesto

1/3 C. chopped sun-dried tomatoes
1/4 C. crumbled herbed feta cheese
1 frozen puff pastry sheet, thawed, cut in half

Directions

1. Set your oven at 375 degrees F before doing anything else.
2. Coat chicken breasts with a mixture of mashed garlic and egg yolk in a glass dish before covering it up with a plastic wrap and refrigerating these chicken breasts for at least four hours.
3. Put ½ of the spinach in the center of half of a pastry and then place one piece of chicken breast over it before adding 1 table spoon pesto, sun-dried tomatoes, feta cheese and then the remaining spinach.
4. Wrap it up with the other half of the pastry.
5. Repeat the same steps for the remaining breast pieces.
6. Place all these on a baking dish.
7. Bake in the preheated oven for about 40 minutes or until the chicken is tender.
8. Serve.

Open Pie
Herbs and Salami

Prep Time: 15 mins
Total Time: 1 hr

Servings per Recipe: 8
Calories   155 kcal
Carbohydrates   3.7 g
Cholesterol   39 mg
Fat   12.2 g
Protein   7.7 g
Sodium   253 mg

Ingredients

3/4 tsp chopped fresh parsley
1 clove garlic, minced
1 tsp dried rosemary
1 tsp dried thyme
1 tsp dried marjoram
2 oz thinly sliced salami, chopped

1 (2.2 lb) wheel Brie cheese
1 sheet frozen puff pastry, thawed
water
1 egg, beaten

Directions

1. Set your oven at 350 degrees F before doing anything else.
2. Spread a mixture of parsley, marjoram, garlic, rosemary, thyme and salami over one half of vertically sliced brie before placing the other half on top.
3. Now place this in the center of a puff pastry and fold it up before brushing the pastry with beaten eggs.
4. Bake this in the preheated oven for about 30 minutes or until golden brown.
5. Cool it down a little.
6. Serve

FRIED
Calzone

Prep Time: 20 mins
Total Time: 2 hrs 20 mins

Servings per Recipe: 12
Calories	528 kcal
Carbohydrates	21.4 g
Cholesterol	33 mg
Fat	46.2 g
Protein	8 g
Sodium	169 mg

Ingredients

4 1/2 cups all-purpose flour
1 1/2 tsps salt
1/2 cup shortening
1 1/4 cups water, or as needed
2 tbsps olive oil
1 small onion, chopped
1 1/2 pounds ground beef
1 pinch salt
2 tbsps paprika

1 tbsp cumin
1/2 tsp ground black pepper
1/2 cup raisins
1 tbsp white vinegar
2 hard-cooked eggs, peeled and chopped
1 quart oil for frying, or as needed

Directions

1. Mix salt, flour and sliced shortening very thoroughly before adding water and turning all this into a ball shaped dough to be put into refrigerator wrapped in plastic wrap.
2. Cook onion in hot oil for a few minutes before adding beef, salt, paprika, cumin and black pepper, and cook until beef is brown before adding vinegar and raisins.
3. Cool it down before adding some hard cooked eggs into it.
4. Make 2 inch balls out of dough and after rolling it up on a floured surface; put some meat into it before folding it into half-moon shapes.
5. Deep fry one or two at a time for about 5 minutes
6. Serve.

Pumpkin
Calzone with Cloves

Prep Time: 20 mins
Total Time: 1 hr

Servings per Recipe: 12

Calories	384 kcal
Carbohydrates	52.3 g
Cholesterol	46 mg
Fat	18.6 g
Protein	5.5 g
Sodium	710 mg

Ingredients

3 cups all-purpose flour
1/3 cup white sugar
1 1/2 tsps salt
1/4 tsp baking powder
1 cup vegetable shortening
1 cup warm water
4 cups canned pure pumpkin
2 eggs
1 cup white sugar

1 tsp salt
1 1/2 tsps ground cinnamon
1 tsp ground ginger
1/2 tsp ground cloves
1 beaten egg

Directions

1. Set your oven to 350 degrees F before doing anything else.
2. Mix flour, salt, sugar and shortening in a large sized bowl before adding water with the help of a spoon continuously until you see that dough is formed.
3. Roll it up on the floured surface before cutting it into 12 equal parts.
4. Make twelve balls out of it and cover it up until you make the filling.
5. Whisk pumpkin, cinnamon, 2 eggs, 1 tsp of salt, ginger, 1 cup of sugar and cloves in a bowl until smooth before filling the dough ball with this and folding it up to make half-moon shaped calzone.
6. Press the edges with the help of a folk before placing it on the baking sheet.
7. Brush all these calzones with the beaten egg before baking it for about 20 minutes or until you see that the top of each calzone has turned brown.
8. Serve

APRICOT
Calzones

Prep Time: 30 mins
Total Time: 1 hr

Servings per Recipe: 12

Calories	249 kcal
Carbohydrates	42.7 g
Cholesterol	0 mg
Fat	8.2 g
Protein	3.3 g
Sodium	133 mg

Ingredients

4 cups chopped dried apricots
1 1/2 cups water
3/4 cup white sugar
1 tsp ground cinnamon
1 tsp ground allspice
1 pinch ground cloves
1 (.25 ounce) envelope active dry yeast
1 cup lukewarm water
1/4 cup shortening or butter

3 cups all-purpose flour
1 tsp salt
1 quart oil for frying, or as needed

Directions

1. Bring a mixture of apricots and water to boil and cook for about 15 minutes before setting it aside.

2. Blend apricots, sugar, cinnamon, allspice, cloves and some water in a blender until smooth.

3. Let the mixture of yeast and water stand for about five minutes before adding water, flour and shortening to make dough.

4. Knead this dough for about eight minutes to get it smooth and elastic before rolling it up on a floured surface and cutting circles using a cookie cutter.

5. Fill these cookie-shaped circles with the filling before folding it up and pressing the edges with your finger.

6. Deep fry these calzones in hot oil until you see that they are golden brown from both sides.

7. Serve

Calzone
of Beef and Black Beans

Prep Time: 15 mins
Total Time: 40 mins

Servings per Recipe: 10

Calories	290 kcal
Carbohydrates	25.8 g
Cholesterol	56 mg
Fat	14.7 g
Protein	13.9 g
Sodium	569 mg

Ingredients

1 tbsp vegetable oil
1 pound ground beef or turkey
1 medium onion, chopped
1/2 tsp salt
1 (10.75 ounce) can Campbell's®
Condensed Black Bean, Cumin & Cilantro

Soup
4 ounces queso fresco, crumbled (cheese)
1 (14 ounce) package calzone dough, thawed
1 egg, beaten

Directions

1. Set your oven to 425 degrees F.
2. Cook beef, salt and onion in hot over high heat until you see that the beef is thoroughly browned.
3. Turn down the heat to medium before stirring in soup and cooking it until the mixture is really hot and bubbling.
4. Turn the heat off and add queso fresco before spooning this mixture into the dough circle.
5. Fold up these calzones and place them on the baking sheet.
6. Brush all these calzones with the beaten egg before baking it for about 20 minutes or until you see that the top of each calzone has turned brown.

HAWAIIAN
Butter Calzones

Prep Time: 15 mins
Total Time: 1 hr 15 mins

Servings per Recipe: 12

Calories	292 kcal
Carbohydrates	38.3 g
Cholesterol	41 mg
Fat	14.7 g
Protein	2.5 g
Sodium	115 mg

Ingredients

3 cups white sugar
1 pound butter, softened and cut into pieces
2 (8 ounce) packages cream cheese, softened and cut into pieces

4 cups all-purpose flour
2 (10 ounce) jars pineapple preserves

Directions

1. Set your oven to 425 degrees F.
2. Mix flour and butter very thoroughly before adding cream cheese and kneading this dough until you see that it is no longer crumbly.
3. Make 1 inch balls from this dough and flat it out on a floured surface using rolling pin.
4. Fold it up around 1 tbsp preserve before pressing edges with fingers to seal.
5. Bake it in the preheated oven for about 20 minutes.

Latin
Mushroom Calzone

🥣 Prep Time: 15 mins
🕐 Total Time: 40 mins

Servings per Recipe: 20
Calories	115 kcal
Carbohydrates	11.6 g
Cholesterol	5 mg
Fat	6.3 g
Protein	3.7 g
Sodium	319 mg

Ingredients

3 cups all-purpose flour
2 (7.5 ounce) packages refrigerated buttermilk biscuits (not the layered varieties)
Cornmeal for rolling
2 tbsps olive oil
1 medium onion, finely chopped
2 (10 ounce) packages white mushrooms, stems trimmed, cut into small dice

1 (4.5 ounce) can chopped green chilies
2 large garlic cloves, minced
2 tbsps minced fresh cilantro
Salt and pepper to taste
4 ounces goat cheese, crumbled
Olive oil, for brushing

Directions

1. Set your oven to 450 degrees F.
2. Cook onion in hot oil for about three minutes before adding mushrooms and cooking for another five minutes.
3. Now add chilies, pepper, garlic, salt and cilantro, and cook all this for another two minutes before turning the heat off and adding goat cheese.
4. Place biscuit on the cornmeal-coated surface and sprinkle cornmeal as required before rolling all these into five inch circles.
5. Fill each circle with the filling you just prepared before placing them on the baking sheet
6. Bake it for about 20 minutes or until you see that the top of each calzone has turned brown

QUESO CHANCO
Calzone

Prep Time: 20 mins
Total Time: 40 mins

Servings per Recipe: 12
Calories	343 kcal
Carbohydrates	39 g
Cholesterol	57 mg
Fat	13.8 g
Protein	14.8 g
Sodium	287 mg

Ingredients

3 cups all-purpose flour
1 tsp baking powder
1/2 tsp salt
2 tbsps butter
1 cup whole milk
1 egg, well beaten

1 cup queso chanco (or Swiss cheese or Havarti), cut into 1/2-inch cubes

Directions

1. Set your oven to 375 degrees F.
2. Combine flour, salt, hot milk and baking powder very thoroughly before kneading it until you see that the dough is smooth and elastic.
3. Cut the dough into four inch circles before filling it up with mound of cheese.
4. Press the edges of the calzones with folk before placing them in the baking sheet.
5. Brush all these calzones with the beaten egg before baking it for about 20 minutes or until you see that the top of each calzone has turned brown.
6. Serve

Picadillo
Spanish Calzone

🥣 Prep Time: 15 mins
🕐 Total Time: 40 mins

Servings per Recipe: 20
Calories	140 kcal
Carbohydrates	14.3 g
Cholesterol	13 mg
Fat	6.6 g
Protein	6.4 g
Sodium	313 mg

Ingredients

2 (7.5 ounce) packages refrigerated buttermilk biscuits (not the layered varieties)
Cornmeal for rolling
2 tbsps olive oil
1 medium onion, finely chopped
1/2 medium Granny Smith apple, cut into small dice
1/4 tsp ground cinnamon
1/8 tsp ground cloves
2 cups shredded meat from a rotisserie chicken

1 (16 ounce) can crushed tomatoes
1/4 cup seedless raisins
1/4 cup chopped pimento-stuffed olives
2 large garlic cloves, minced
1/4 cup toasted slivered almonds
Salt and pepper, to taste
Olive oil, for brushing

Directions

1. Set oven to 450 degrees F.
2. Cook onion and apple in hot oil for about four minutes before adding spices and cooking for another 30 seconds.
3. Now add olives, chicken, raisins and tomatoes, and cook for another seven minutes before adding garlic, pepper, almonds and salt.
4. Place biscuit on the cornmeal-coated surface and sprinkle cornmeal as required before rolling all these into five inch circles.
5. Fill each circle with the filling you just prepared before placing them on the baking sheet
6. Bake it for about 20 minutes or until you see that the top of each calzone has turned brown.

ARGENTINA
Calzones

Prep Time: 15 mins
Total Time: 40 mins

Servings per Recipe: 10
Calories   498 kcal
Carbohydrates   27.7 g
Cholesterol   73 mg
Fat   36.8 g
Protein   14.7 g
Sodium   326 mg

Ingredients

1/2 cup shortening
2 onions, chopped
1 pound lean ground beef
2 tsps Hungarian sweet paprika
3/4 tsp hot paprika
1/2 tsp crushed red pepper flakes
1 tsp ground cumin
1 tbsp distilled white vinegar
1/4 cup raisins

1/2 cup pitted green olives, chopped
2 hard-cooked eggs, chopped
salt to taste
1 (17.5 ounce) package frozen puff pastry sheets, thawed

Directions

1. Cook onion and shortening in hot oil for a few minutes before adding sweet paprika, crushed red pepper flakes, hot paprika and salt.

2. Cook meat in boiling water for some time before transferring this to a dish and adding salt, vinegar and cumin.

3. Mix this meat mixture with the onion mixture in a bowl and let it cool down.

4. Cut ten circles from the pastry dough before placing that meat mixture, hard-boiled egg, raisins and olives on each one of them.

5. Now fold it around this filling very neatly to form a shape that resembles half-moon.

6. Press the edges with a folk.

7. Set your oven to 375 degrees F and place these calzones in the baking sheet.

8. Brush all these calzones with the beaten egg before baking it for about 30 minutes or until you see that the top of each calzone has turned brown.

9. Serve.

Central American
Calzones

Prep Time: 30 mins
Total Time: 1 hr

Servings per Recipe: 22
Calories	105 kcal
Carbohydrates	11.7 g
Cholesterol	32 mg
Fat	5.6 g
Protein	2.3 g
Sodium	102 mg

Ingredients

1 recipe pastry for a 9 inch double crust pie
2 large potatoes, peeled and cubed
2 tbsps olive oil
2 onions, diced
3 hard-cooked eggs, chopped

1/4 cup chopped green olives
1/2 cup raisins
salt and pepper to taste
2 eggs, beaten

Directions

1. Set your oven to 375 degrees F.
2. Cook potatoes in boiling water for about five minutes to get it tendered.
3. Cook onion in hot oil for about 5 minutes before adding cooked potatoes and cooking it for another ten minutes or until you see that the potatoes are lightly brown.
4. Transfer this to bowl and stir in raisins, salt, pepper, hard-cooked eggs and olives.
5. Cut ten circles from the pastry dough after rolling it up on a floured surface.
6. Now fold it around this filling very neatly to form a shape that resembles half-moon.
7. Press the edges with a folk and place them in the baking sheet.
8. Brush all these calzones with the beaten egg before baking it for about 30 minutes or until you see that the top of each calzone has turned brown.

19200834R00040